Lord, Help Me...
I'M SiNGLE

by frances leary

TATE PUBLISHING, LLC

"Lord, Help Me . . . I'm Single" by Frances Leary

Copyright © 2005 by Frances Leary. All rights reserved.

Published in the United States of America
by Tate Publishing, LLC
127 East Trade Center Terrace
Mustang, OK 73064
(888) 361–9473

Book design copyright © 2005 by Tate Publishing, LLC. All rights reserved.

No part of this publication may be reproduced, stored in a retrieval system or transmitted in any way by any means, electronic, mechanical, photocopy, recording or otherwise without the prior permission of the author except as provided by USA copyright law.

Scripture quotations are taken from the *Holy Bible, New International Version* ®, Copyright © 1973, 1978, 1984 by International Bible Society. Used by permission of Zondervan Publishing House. All rights reserved.

This book is designed to provide accurate and authoritative information with regard to the subject matter covered. This information is given with the understanding that neither the author nor Tate Publishing, LLC is engaged in rendering legal, professional advice. Since the details of your situation are fact dependent, you should additionally seek the services of a competent professional.

ISBN: 1–5988615–1–4

This book is dedicated to my girlfriends:

Camp Allen girls, Garcia girls, UNT and UH girls, Macaroni girls, Dulles girls, and MUN girls. Thank you for the laughs and inspirations!

Most especially this book is for Anne, my sister and kindred spirit. You've been with me every step of the way, and it's been a blast!

Acknowledgments

    I would like to thank the team at Tate Publishing for the amazing collaborative effort that has made this dream into a reality, especially Trinity Tate for believing in me from the very beginning, Stacy Baker for helping to make my writing the best it can be, Sommer Buss for her brilliant creative designs that so perfectly capture the spirit of this book, and Melanie Harr-Hughes, whose layout brought this book visually to life. God bless you all!
    I would also like to thank Susan Cooper for her preliminary editing efforts throughout my writing process. Without her this book would not be what it is today.
    I want to thank my family for their constant support and devotion to this project, and above all, I wish to extend my thanks to the single girls of the world for being my kindred spirits. Here's to you!

Table of Contents

Foreword 9

Key 10

Dating 11
The Dating Scene
Fending for Myself
It's a Date
Waiting by the Phone
Relationship Regrets

On the Home Front 23
Cooking IQ
Dishwasher Dilemma
Burned
Deceptively Burnt Burger Bites
The Vomiting Vacuum
The Art of Painting
Toilet Troubles

A Look in the Mirror 39
Couch Potato
Phone Frustrations
Finance Fiascos
The Fitness Challenge
New Car
Daring To Dream

Man's Best Friends 53
New Puppy
Larger Than Life
Puppy School
Feline Fits
Dog Owner Don'ts
Tub Time

Around the World 67
The Sardine Sleeper
Read the Label
The Drugstore Language Barrier
The Last Train Ride
Cuban Kayak Crisis

Still Dating 79
Concert Stand-up
The Dr. Jekyll/Mr. Hyde Date
Bingo Blues
Love Letter
Broken Heart

Friends and Family 91
Wedding Worries
Birthday Blues
Catching a Lie
Sister of the Bride
True Love

A Bend in the Road 103
Saying Goodbyes
A New Home
A Smiling Stranger
Looking Back

Foreword

Frances' creative imagination was evident when, as a toddler, she played with the family of blue rabbits in her closet. Her belief in the angel friend who visited when her parents were away only hinted at the faith that would soon allow such a young child to place her praying hands upon a friend's knee and see it healed. Since then, she has grown into the delightful young woman whose life as a single Christian is reflected so truthfully in these pages.

Lord, Help Me . . . I'm Single is a treasury of events in Frances' life. It is funny, sad, poignant, and silly. It involves soul-searching as she strives to learn from each occurrence. Above all, it takes her, and the reader, beyond the obvious to the search for what God would have her learn each time.

God has blessed us with her presence in our lives. May you be richly blessed as you journey with Frances through her life as a single person.

Susan Cooper

Key

Lovely! = Not lovely!

Holy cow! = Oh, my goodness!

Yikes! = Holy cow!

Good night! = Yikes!

Ugh! = Disgusting!

Mmm! = Not tasty at all!

Aaaahhh! = What am I going to do?/Yikes!

Hmmm . . . = Not quite sure what to make of this . . .

Dating

"*There is a time for everything, and a season for every activity under heaven: a time to be born and a time to die, a time to plant and a time to uproot, a time to kill and a time to heal, a time to tear down and a time to build, a time to weep and a time to laugh, a time to mourn and a time to dance, a time to scatter stones and a time to gather them, a time to embrace and a time to refrain, a time to search and a time to give up, a time to keep and a time to throw away, a time to tear and a time to mend, a time to be silent and a time to speak, a time to love and a time to hate, a time for war and a time for peace.*"
Ecclesiastes 3:1–8

Lord, I can't help but wonder when it will be my time . . . my time to love. I have so much love to give, and I do so want to share it. Father God, please help me to treasure my times that are now. It is my time to be with friends, my time to meet new people, my time to learn about myself, my time to be with myself. Lord, thank you for this time.

• Frances Leary •

The Dating Scene

It is a scary scene out there. No, I'm not talking horror film scary, but it's rather frightening nonetheless. "Hey, Hot Mama" and "Hey, Babe," while somewhat feeding my ego, are not introductions that have led me to the man of my dreams. Do you know that I actually heard the line "What's happenin', Hot Stuff?" one night? That's when I knew I needed a change of scenery. Dating has become more about sex than really getting to know another person. Sex is almost always expected when people begin to see each other. If I say "yes" to a date, it is often assumed that I am saying "yes" to sex. Not only that, but even when I'm not on a date (which, sadly to say, is quite frequently), it's often difficult to go out without colliding with sexual innuendoes everywhere. It is not supposed to work that way! As a Christian, I believe sex is meant to be special between two people whom God has chosen to bring together. I know there are other Christians out there who feel the same way, but I am definitely not finding them around town. Could it be that perhaps I am looking in the wrong places?

Please guide me to the right places, Lord, so that I may find some of those wonderful, Christian men You want me to know. In the meantime, please keep me strong. Be with me as I spend time with men

• Dating •

and enable me to stand by my values. Give me the strength to say "no" and the judgment to know which men value me for my beliefs and character. Help me never to sell myself short by equating physical intimacy with love. God, You are with me always, and I give myself to You that You may guide my every decision in life.

Fending for Myself

A friend of mine from church has been asking me out for a while now, so I finally agreed to give it a go. He's a great guy, and we always have a good time. I'm just not sure there's anything else there. Anyway—he planned for us to go to dinner and a movie. Good, solid plan—what could go wrong? He picked me up before dinner and honked from the car for me to come out. Not even a knock on the door. Okay, I'm not Miss Manners, but isn't that pushing the limit just a bit on a first date? I was somewhat annoyed, but I decided to brush it off and not let it spoil a potentially lovely time. He drove to Chili's for dinner; not too creative, but it always gets the job done right. We chatted over dinner—quite nice, actually. To my surprise, I was having a good time. The server delivered our check, and to my chagrin, my date made no move to locate his wallet. I sat there, finishing my drink and wondering to myself just what I should do. I assumed we would split the check, since he did not grab it immediately. Not too romantic, but whatever. I asked about the time of the movie, hoping that would be a subtle hint that perhaps we should pay the check. Well, he responded to my movie question but still made no move—and the movie was supposed to start in 20 minutes. I figured perhaps he was just waiting to make sure I was finished eating. Yes, that had to be it, so I indicated I was

• Dating •

ready to go. Still nothing. Then I did the only thing I could do. I started fishing around in my purse for my wallet. When I found it, he'd still made no move. What? Was he going to sit there and let me pay for both of our meals after he had asked me out? Apparently so. I paid and we left. Did he even notice? By that time, I was rather perturbed with the evening. I began to think of excuses as to why I needed to skip the movie. Too late—we were there. He opened the door to the theater, walked in before me, and proceeded to wait at the snack station, leaving me to buy the tickets. Nice. After I got the tickets, I found him waiting for me with one drink—a Coke for himself. I don't even like Coke! I tried to let myself enjoy the movie, but the horrors of the evening got the best of me. To top it off, he slammed my finger in the car door at the end of the night. What a disaster!

Lord, perhaps I should listen to my instincts. Something told me we weren't going to be a romantic match, and I should have paid attention. I know that You are that voice inside of me; please help me to follow Your guidance in this and all areas of my life. Help me to let go of this experience and keep my friend. A bad date is not a reason to lose a good friend.

It's a Date

I just went out with this really fun, exciting, intelligent man. Wow! Not only that, but he paid for everything. He even opened doors and let me walk in first. Holy cow! Chivalry isn't dead after all. We drove to a delightful restaurant, and after poring over the extensive menu, I ordered what was the most delicious grilled salmon I have ever tasted. The conversation was completely enjoyable, and there was not one awkward moment. How rare! After dinner we walked across the street to a jazz club and listened to a wonderful jazz pianist play the night away. We danced and enjoyed the music while we talked about life. He was perfectly chivalrous the entire evening. I was beginning to think there were no gentlemen in existence. I like it when God shows me I am wrong about those kinds of things. Who knows what is in store for us, but I would like to have the opportunity to get to know this new person in my life. I feel all bubbly inside, like a girl home from her first school dance. I would like to treasure this feeling for just a little while. So I'm off to bed to dream of romance that thrives in the 21st-century Camelot I witnessed tonight.

Lord, thank You for this little bit of extra spice in my life. Please help me to follow Your will for me

• Dating •

in this and all situations. Whether I have many more dates with him or none, help me to remember the good time we had together. He helped restore a confidence in me that I am attractive and enjoyable to be around. Give me the ability to hold onto that whether I am with someone or alone.

• Frances Leary •

• Dating •

Waiting by the Phone

No, no, no, I am not just sitting here by the phone for fun. I am willing it to ring. Ring, ring, ring! Does that work? I know that most of us at some point or another have done it, and in my experience it does not seem to be that effective. However, I keep hoping that my experience will prove wrong this time. Why did I have the opportunity to go out with someone I thought was such a great guy if he is not going to call me? He said he would call. I am not a demanding woman, but I do believe that people should do what they say. He said he would call today. I know he is busy, but he should not have . . . Oh, the phone just rang. Maybe??? No, it was my parents. Isn't that nice? No, I mean, that is nice, but that is not the call I was waiting for at the moment. Anyway, as I was saying, he should not have said it if he had no intention of following through. I almost wish we hadn't gone on the date at all. That way I wouldn't be waiting here with anticipation for what might never come. I suppose I am a bit aggravated, but I cannot seem to shake the confidence that we both had a great time on our date. I know it was not just me. I know it. Right?

Lord, help me to be patient. If this is a good man with whom You want me to spend time, I know it will work out that way. If not, will You please give me a big hug so that I know there will be someone great for me one day? Actually, will You give me a hug anyway? Thank You, God. Your hugs are the best I could ever ask for.

• Dating •

Relationship Regrets

I made a mistake last night. Not too long ago, a friend of mine introduced me to someone—a man, that is. No, not the same one who had me sitting by the phone. I realized with that one that I don't want to be with someone who doesn't treat me with respect, but it seems that I still have so many things to learn. This new guy—we felt an attraction at first. We talked on the phone, e-mailed—all the things you do when you are beginning to have feelings for someone. Something changed last night. In all truthfulness, I knew it all along. I never waited by the phone for his calls, I never looked forward to hearing his voice, I never anticipated seeing him in the evenings, and I certainly never encountered him in my dreams. I knew. I knew that this relationship was not right; although we both walked through the pre-relationship steps, my walk remained slow-paced and monotonous. It was as if I were going through a motion I knew I was supposed to go through. I thought I had explained myself to him, and I understood that we both felt the same way. We decided to go on as friends without pursuing the romantic aspect further. What a relief! Well, as friends we went to dinner last night. It was a lovely evening until he kissed me. It became even worse when I kissed him back. With that kiss, I not only deceived myself, but I deceived him as well.

Lord God, forgive me for allowing myself to sink to the belief that I need someone else to make my life complete. I know that only You can complete me. Forgive me for leading this young man to think that I had feelings that were not there. You revealed my heart to me much earlier in our relationship. Forgive me for giving into physical desires, and please help me to be true to the purity You have created within me. Most of all, God, please help me to forgive myself.

On the Home Front

"Jesus said, 'Therefore everyone who hears these words of mine and puts them into practice is like a wise man who built his house on the rock. The rain came down, the streams rose, and the winds blew and beat against that house; yet it did not fall, because it had its foundation on the rock. But everyone who hears these words of mine and does not put them into practice is like a foolish man who built his house on sand. The rain came down, the streams rose, and the winds blew and beat against that house, and it fell with a great crash.'"

Matthew 7:24–27

Father God, as I make a home for myself and learn to take care of it, I ask that You be its foundation. Come into my house, Lord, and abide in it as You abide in me. It is Your love that so completely fills my house.

Cooking IQ

You know what? I really hate cooking for myself. Perhaps at least some of you singles out there can relate. First of all, I do not know how. Second, I always have food left over for at least a week, so I have to eat it. That is just slightly monotonous. Then when I don't eat it because I'm tired of the repetition, I find it weeks later at the back of my refrigerator in some sealed container overflowing with mold. Lovely! Then I have to choose between washing the container with the mold and just throwing it out. Come on, which would you do? Of course, all that happens only when I actually do cook. It is so much easier to order out or pick up something on the way home. This is not good. It costs money, it is often not healthy, it promotes my lazy behavior, and I still find the leftovers at the back of the refrigerator a week later. At least there's no decision to make about whether to keep the container. I am, however, making some good friendships with the young people working at the takeout windows. I'm not sure whether that is a valid justification—I think not. I know I need to discipline myself to cook more, but it gets discouraging when the only thing I can cook well is scrambled eggs.

Lord, give me the patience to learn to cook and

• On the Home Front •

the desire to want to do it. If I could actually make things I like, I do not think eating at home would be so bad. Since I am only cooking for myself, I can make anything I like. Help me to have positive feelings about it, God. I know You are with me in the kitchen and everywhere else.

• Frances Leary •

Dishwasher Dilemma

Okay, so this is the scenario. For three or four days I have been procrastinating about doing the dishes. I know, how irresponsible of me, but I can probably list washing dishes as one of the things I least enjoy doing. I hate unloading the dishwasher, so I cram absolutely every dish possible into the machine before I run it. Well, as I arrived home this evening, I discovered that if I wanted to eat on something other than the lid to my boiling pot, I would be forced to run and unload the dishwasher. My disgruntled hesitation finally gave way when I remembered that I had several errands to run before I could eat anyway. Perfect! Just enough time to wash the dishes. Well, then I was presented with another dilemma. As I reached into the cabinet and grabbed the box of dishwasher powder, it felt rather light. Upon examination I realized that I had neglected to replace it with a new box the last time I visited the store. *No problem*, I thought to myself. I'll just use a small dab of this liquid dishwashing soap—no, not the dishwasher kind—just the kind one might use rinsing out dishes in the sink. After all, they both serve the same purpose. What could possibly go wrong? That, my fellow single, was the wrong question. Apparently, no one had ever invited me into the Dishwasher Club because when I returned home from my errands, the entire floor of

• On the Home Front •

my kitchen was engulfed in bubbles. No, actually it was not just my floor. Standing a full 5'5", I was surrounded by suds reaching up to my chest. Perfect, if I wanted a clothed bath. By the time the cleaning was done, the last thing I wanted to do was cook dinner to eat on my sparkly clean dishes. So I ordered Chinese.

Lord, thank You for humility. Times like these remind me that I am always learning. Forgive me for any passing remarks about all the older women I know who should have told me long ago about the dishwasher detergent rule. In passing, we often say and think things we later regret. Help me always to hold onto my sense of humor so that, in times of troubles or in times of bubbles, I can always look on the bright side.

Burned

Well, I made my first casserole this evening. You know how I feel about cooking, so this was a major step. I spent an hour at the grocery store choosing just the right ingredients along with items that would complement my dinner. I can't seem simply to go into the store, get what's on the list, and come out. I always discover some delightful treat that I must have, like the chocolate turtle cheesecake brownies I thought would go superbly well with my casserole. It then took me two hours to combine all of the ingredients and place them in the pan correctly. Two hours. Apparently, there is order to these kinds of things. You can't just toss it all together and expect it to be tasty. No, one must layer appropriately in order to have the desired result. After following the recipe precisely up to this point, everything was going well. So far, so good. Now the easy part. I just had to let it bake. However, as it came closer to the time to remove the casserole from the oven, a somewhat distasteful aroma began to fill the air. Yes, after only a moment's time I discovered that my labor of love was burning in the oven. Actually, I do not believe that burning is a strong enough word. What appeared in the oven seemed to be in the same pan as my casserole, but it was charred through and through. Mmmm! There is just nothing quite so tasty as casserole burnt to a crisp. I suppose I could peel off all the edges and spoon out the slightly less charred inside, but that just doesn't sound too appetizing. I think I will be ordering pizza.

Lord, help me to have the perseverance to keep trying, even though it is discouraging when I fail. Every failure is turned into a success if it is a learning experience. Well, I learned that it is important, while cooking, to check the oven every so often. What a novel idea. See, God, it is a success, and I will keep cooking until I get it right (at least most of it).

Deceptively Burnt Burger Bites

I was so excited that my grandmother was coming to visit that I think I might have overextended myself. I offered to cook for her. I know, I know—what was I thinking? Once my brief excitement wore off, I was stricken with complete panic. Ahhhh! What would I do? Okay, okay, think. . . . There must be something that I could not possibly ruin. Hamburgers! How hard could hamburgers be? Little did I know. Guests for dinner included my grandmother, my sister, and me. I think my sister was already a bit wary of my cooking by now, but she chose to stick by me in my efforts. To this day, she knows that was a mistake. In the absence of a grill, I opted to cook the burgers in a sauté pan on the stovetop. *No problem*, I thought to myself. I bought the already shaped patties, and I was ready to go. Add a little seasoning and turn on the stove. So far, so good. However, apparently one has to adjust the temperature setting for different foods—who knew? Not me, of course. Thinking they were done, since they appeared to be fairly well charred on each side, I served my meal. Yummy. We all applied our condiments of choice, and my sister was the first to try a bite. Well, I got the hint that perhaps something was amiss when red liquid oozed from her mouth. Ahhh—raw on the inside. How lovely. My grandmother bravely tried hers, but the result was no better. I threw them back into the pan, but since they were already burnt on the outside, they never really did achieve the right taste. We ate lots of dessert that night (which thankfully I had bought). Chocolate pie to the rescue.

Lord, again I find myself discouraged by my attempts at cooking. Please help me to keep trying. Only my diligence can help me learn. Thank You for helping me to have faith that one day even I might be a good cook.

• Frances Leary •

The Vomiting Vacuum

Have you ever spent time pondering the miraculous nature of a vacuum? No, I imagine not. Nor had I, until I was forced to do it one day. I had pulled out my great-aunt's old Hoover, and although I knew it would not do amazing justice to the floors, it was my only option since company was on its way. I had almost completed the living room floor when I was halted in my steps by an earsplitting POOF! All at once, I looked like a chimney sweep, and I discovered that the vacuum bag had explosively regurgitated its entire contents on the living room floor and me. Apparently, it is necessary to change the vacuum bag every once in a while to ensure proper working order. I don't know how I thought a vacuum worked. Perhaps I thought it magically turned dirt into air. Maybe I thought the dirt was destroyed by the electronic fields as it passed from the vacuum through the covered wires of the cord into the wall. There could be a storage place inside the wall for the dirt after it gets sucked through the vacuum. Obviously, none of these scenarios is the case, and no, I didn't actually believe any of them. I had simply never seriously pondered vacuum upkeep. Needless to say, I do not have Mary Poppins' practically perfect magic skills and thus was left to clean the extraordinary mess with my own two hands. Ironically, the perfect

• On the Home Front •

item for the job was the vacuum.

Thank You, Lord, for allowing me to find humor in the scrapes I seem to face every day. Thank You, too, for the humor of my friends. I think life would be so much less enjoyable if I could not laugh at myself and the silly situations that surround me. Please help me to continue to laugh and smile and enjoy life with all its surprises.

The Art of Painting

My mother and father generously offered to help me paint my new apartment. I had never spent time perfecting my painting skills, so I was very grateful for their assistance. We began with a base coat primer, and Dad got out the paint gun saying it would speed up the process. It sped it up, all right, and it painted where we didn't even know we needed paint. The entire carpet received a generous speckled coat, and the highlighting job it did on my hair was one of a kind. Thank goodness, we hadn't moved in the furniture. We decided against using the paint gun for the second coat, so we got started the following day with rollers and brushes. How hard can it be, right? Yeah! That's just what I was thinking when I heard a shriek from my mother. Apparently, she had spilled the majority of her paint tray on the stairs. Hey, that's okay. After all, the spill simply connected the dots from the day before. Might as well give the carpet a little bit of color. We cleaned up the spill as best we could and continued with the task at hand. My father excused himself to make a phone call, and as he did, he warned me about the paint tray that was now sitting on the floor. I nodded, thinking, *Duh, of course I'll be careful*. Apparently my overconfidence was my downfall. No sooner had Dad picked up the phone than I stepped back to survey my job. Where did I step? Of course, I did—directly in the paint. My entire foot was engulfed in milky blue liquid; it was like making a mold of my foot. Well, that did it. We all broke out in hysterics and laughed until we couldn't laugh anymore. It was a comedy of errors, and we all played a part. Thank goodness for fingernail polish remover. I wouldn't recommend that you try our painting methods, but just in case you do, polish remover is great for getting paint out of carpet.

Lord, thank You for Your constant reminders that I'm not perfect. It's also comforting to know that no one else is perfect either. We all make mistakes, and I thank You for helping us laugh at ourselves. Thank You for my parents; I treasure them even on the messy days. These are the times we remember, Lord. Thank You for that.

• Frances Leary •

• On the Home Front •

Toilet Troubles

Well, today was just classic. Perhaps these types of things should be kept private, but come on—if I can help one single be more prepared than I, then I have accomplished my mission. My new landlord had warned me of pipe trouble in the apartment. "Make sure not to get hair into the drain, blah, blah, blah," but I wasn't prepared for this. I must admit to being a proponent of excessive toilet paper use. I mean, really, who wants to cut corners in that department? Well, apparently I should change my tactics. There I was in my newly painted bathroom barely escaping the exploding toilet. Lovely! This was not the worst thing, however. The worst was that I had not yet purchased a plunger for my new home. Ahhh! I said a quick prayer of thanks for Wal-Mart's late business hours and set out on my mission. However, what I thought would be a simple five-minute purchase became much more complicated. The store was out of complete toilet plungers. They had the plunger parts but no handles to connect. Hmmm. How does that work? Well, since I didn't have the option of going to another store and was sure I would need the use of my toilet before the next day, I had to find something workable out of these choices. I selected a large accordion-looking plunger, thinking it would be easier to use without a handle. In hindsight, I'm not sure my logic was of any benefit. Anyway, I returned home promptly and got to work. Hmmm—what could I use? Since I didn't have a handy stack of wooden handles, I opted for the broom. No duct tape? I decided that transparent tape (you know—the kind you use to wrap presents) should do just fine. I did my best to tape the broom stick to the top of the accordion plunger. Gobs and gobs of tape later, I was ready to begin the task at hand. Without going into graphic detail, the job finally got done after the handle slipped off the plunger about a dozen times. What a disaster. The moral of this story: Be prepared!

Father God, I appreciate You teaching me humility. I also realize now that I truly must be prepared for small disasters to happen around the house. I don't know whether the lesson had to be such a messy one, but I'm grateful just the same. Please help me to be prepared, and give me the strength to handle all the surprises that come my way.

A Look in the Mirror

". . . for it is God who works in you to will and to act according to his good purpose."
Philippians 2:13

Dearest Father, I pray that my thoughts and words, my actions and meditations may all glorify You. Thank You for guiding me, body, mind, and soul, to do Your will in my life. I pray that I may honor You with all that I am and all that I do. I fall short so often, but You forgive me, restore me, and fill me with Your spirit. Thank You for helping me to glorify You.

Couch Potato

Ahhhh! I have become a couch potato. This is a very scary thing. I find myself coming home in the evenings, placing my bottom on the sofa, and not removing it until the prime-time shows are over. Good night! Not only that, but my fingers are becoming much too familiar with the remote control. I promised myself I would never be this way. Perhaps I am exaggerating just a tad, but I definitely do have those days. They seem to be coming more and more, and sometimes it is very hard to fight my lack of motivation. I finish all my work before I get home, and then I am all to myself. To a point this is good, but I need to use that time wisely. I am reminded of the Shel Silverstein poem in which a little boy who watches so much television actually becomes the TV. I would hate to find myself caught in an old wives' tale where I am frozen in a permanent position because my habit was too forming. I can just see it now—my bottom widening into a sofa (hopefully, just a loveseat), my arms stretching into antennas, and my head squaring off to make me the center of attention in the living room. Somehow, I don't think that would get me many dates. Okay—so I'm being ridiculous, but isn't it almost as ridiculous to waste my entire evening, every evening, on the couch?

• A Look in the Mirror •

Lord God, help me to put down the remote control and become more motivated when I am at home alone. Inspire me with the desire to use my mind creatively, even in my off-work hours. Lord, thank You for this down time that You have given me in the evenings. I want to use every bit of it to glorify You.

• Frances Leary •

Phone Frustrations

There I was. For one night I had abandoned my couch potato position in exchange for an evening curled up with a favorite novel. Perhaps the thought that I might receive a call from an old high school friend (that I used to date, by the way) had me in a romantically nostalgic mood. Memories passed through my mind, intertwining with the images born through the words of a great writer. I soared on the edge of my imagination, so electrified, so entranced, so . . . Then it happened. The phone rang. Old friend? No. Parents? No. It was not even a person. It was one of those lovely computer survey phone calls. Aaaahhh! Of course, I hung up the phone. That response must not have sent the correct message because seconds later the phone rang again. Guess who? Yes, the computer. A computer! How can I possibly value the importance of speaking on the phone to a robot asking questions that seem totally inconsequential? Yes, I know it is someone's job to find out odd information, but I just cannot appreciate it all the time. If it is not a computer call, it is the phone company wanting me to switch or an organization asking for donations. None of these are bad things, but I often find myself quite annoyed. That caller ID gizmo is looking better and better every day.

• A Look in the Mirror •

Lord, since I cannot ask You to limit all my calls to personal ones, please give me the patience to deal with all calls that come. Help me to recognize that everyone at the other end of my phone is calling for a reason, and I should respect that reason. I think I will enjoy every day better if I take things as they come and consider all that crosses my path important.

• Frances Leary •

Finance Fiascos

Yes, I did it again. I bounced another check. Everyone knows what that means: twenty dollars to the bank and twenty dollars to the store where I wrote the check. This seems to be working backwards. I just cannot seem to get a handle on balancing my budget. I am so accustomed to receiving help from my parents that it has been quite an adjustment to live without it. I am making a decent amount of money, but my spending habits are outrageous. I still want to go out and play like I did in college, but now that money has to pay off my college debts. Shopping excursions are the worst temptation. How can anyone shop without purchasing something? Then once I buy one thing, I seem to need something to coordinate with it. Not only do I purchase items for myself, but I also go overboard with gifts for friends. I thoroughly enjoy giving to people, so I do it much too frequently and extravagantly. I suppose my eating habits don't help the situation at all. I love to eat out! Not only do I wander to fast food and takeout places because I can't cook, but I have an irresistible passion for good food. I can't cook it, but I love to eat it. Mexican, Italian, Asian, you name it . . . I love it all! I recognize that all of this is contributing to my poor money management, but I cannot seem to control it. I know what I need to do; I'm just not

• A Look in the Mirror •

doing it.

Lord, help me to live in obedience to You by living within my own means. Give me the desire to curtail my spending and use money wisely. Life will be much more enjoyable without worrying about debts. Less spending equals more savings, and that sounds like a very good deal. Thank You for teaching me to be thrifty.

The Fitness Challenge

It appears that in this world, there is a great deal of emphasis on looking good. One only has to glance at the magazine rack in the grocery store or turn on the television to see that almost every person in the public eye is exquisitely trim and fit, in addition to being unimaginably beautiful. It's almost enough to make this average single woman nauseated. Somehow, this fitness and beauty craze seems to contradict many things, for instance what tastes good—fettuccini alfredo, four-cheese pizza, nacho chips smothered in queso, turtle cheesecake . . . I could go on and on and find an unending list of fabulous foods that make very unhealthy contributions to my thighs. (Obviously, I'm not talking about my own cooking here.) Nevertheless, I am finding that it is quite important to me that I look good. No, I'm not attempting to end up on the cover of *Vogue*, and I don't just mean that I want to be pretty. I mean that I want to look healthy and in control of my body. Actually, I am discovering that the better I look, the better I feel. My attitude about myself is improving, and I am not so worried about acquiring health problems when I get older. I think we put emphasis on looking good for the wrong reasons. Everyone should want to look their best so they can feel their best and be healthy—NOT to impress others. Putting on those

• A Look in the Mirror •

running shoes every morning is not always a pleasant thought, but it keeps me disciplined and feeling good (just a tad sweaty). Okay, so I've never gotten up early in my life, but I suppose there's a first for everything.

Lord God, help me to remain obedient to Your will that I take care of my body. Give me the wisdom to stay healthy for the right reasons and not for the sake of others. Forgive my laziness, and strengthen my desire to maintain discipline in this and all areas of my life.

• Frances Leary •

New Car

WOW! Today I did the most adult thing I have ever done. I bought a car. Yes, I've had a car before, but it was the last one left on the lot when my drive-a-heap car broke down. It was cheap, and it was available. Without a doubt I was thankful for having the car, but until now I had not gone through the entire process of purchasing the car of my dreams. I picked it out, I wrote the down-payment check, I signed the papers, and I received the very-low-interest loan. Quite exciting. I have to say she's a beauty. She's a gorgeous green Mustang, and I think I'll name her Jo. She is definitely a girl, of course, because all my cars are girls. On one hand, I'm so proud of myself. On the other, I can't help thinking that my time frame isn't quite what it should be. Just as my friends are getting married, buying houses, and having babies, I finally get around to purchasing an automobile—something most of them accomplished quite some time ago. Oh, well. I don't care. I love my car, and I love it most because it's mine and God helped me find it. I prayed for a long time, and He showed me when the time was right. I suppose He'll show me about all those other things too—when the time is right.

Thank You, Lord, for Your guidance. Thank

• A Look in the Mirror •

You for helping me discern what is right in this and so many other situations. Help me not to compare my life to that of others. Help me to have faith that since You have given me this beautiful life, You will reveal what to do with it, just as You brought me to my car. And it's a great car. Thanks for that too.

• Frances Leary •

Daring To Dream

A dream came true today. Wow! For the past three years I have been singing in a band with two friends (male friends, I might add). We sing Christian worship music and write music that I can only classify as acoustic rock with a Christian flare. While this has been a hobby for all of us, it has been so much more: an outlet to express my passion for music, a challenge to grow as a musician, an opportunity for fellowship with two amazing and solid Christians who keep me accountable. They have become two of the strongest kindred spirits in my life. Our practices are filled with music, of course, but even more special to me have been the many moments filled with laughing and crying, listening to and offering advice, facing obstacles, and overcoming them together. I must admit that I did most of the crying, but I am so thankful that my two band members have understood. I think we have learned a great deal from each other. I know for certain that my knowledge about men has grown significantly over the time I have spent with my two male counterparts, and I hope that I have presented them with some insight into women as well. After three years of creating music together, we went into the studio several months ago to record. What an experience! It was challenging beyond belief, and if you think I cried in practices, just imagine the stu-

• A Look in the Mirror •

dio—the stress, the aim of perfection, the total exposure of all mistakes and flaws. I shed more than my share of tears, I'm sure, but when I look down and see in my hand the result of all our labor, I know it was more than worth it. Our CD in my hand—wow! Our music—lyrics we composed, melodies we shaped, arrangements we wove together—playing not only in my CD player, but forever in my head and in my heart. I pray that our music may also play in the hearts of others.

Father God, thank You for enabling me to live into a dream. Thank You for my two friends and collaborators; their talents have inspired me, and their friendships have made me stronger. Thank You for walking with us and guiding us to realize this dream, and thank You for using us as messengers to deliver the spirit of Your love to others through our music. This entire experience has been a blessing from You.

Man's Best Friends

"And God said 'Let the land produce living creatures according to their kinds: livestock, creatures that move along the ground, and wild animals, each according to its kind.' And it was so. God made the wild animals according to their kinds, the livestock according to their kinds, and all the creatures that move along the ground according to their kinds. And God saw that it was good."

Genesis 1:24–25

Thank You, dear Lord, for the precious gift of animals. Not only am I blessed each and every day by the creatures I witness in the world outside my own doors, but I also take delight in the three treasures that You have placed in my care. They are a source of constant love and devotion, and their love is unconditional. I pray that my love for them may be as unconditional as their love for me.

• Frances Leary •

• Man's Best Friends •

New Puppy

I just got a puppy today. He is so precious and truly a gift from God. He is six weeks old and fits in the palm of my hand. I don't think I've ever seen a puppy this small. He's absolutely darling. Even as small as he is, his dark brown eyes are huge and full of excitement. I think there's a look of happiness swimming around in there, but I can't tell for sure. I hope so. His head is much too large for his body, and he's still not superbly coordinated with his movements yet. His heart beats so quickly, and his delightful puppy kisses absolutely prove how precious he is. I bought him from the SPCA, and he is supposed to be some sort of beagle and terrier mix. His owner had abandoned him, and my heart saddens to think that people could so thoughtlessly discard such a beautiful and loving creature. None of that matters now. I think it's good that he won't remember where he came from. He'll only know that he's mine and that I love him. I am so thankful I arrived at the right time to discover him. Actually, I am certain that God brought me to that place for us to find each other. He should be the perfect size for my apartment, eventually about 20 pounds.

Lord, thank You for this special bundle of joy. Give me all the love in the world to share with him, and keep me disciplined so I can be a good mom for my puppy. I know we will have lots of good adventures, and I hope they will all make You smile.

• Man's Best Friends •

Larger Than Life

Do you remember that puppy I was so thankful for a couple of months ago? Well, he is seven months old now and a total of 43 pounds. Yes, that's right, 43 pounds. Not 20, like they said—43! Okay, so this is a little bit more than I bargained for. He is quite sweet and very smart, but he drives me absolutely crazy. He is so big that he knocks me down when he jumps, not to mention the fact that his nails are quite sharp and dig into my skin when he attacks me. And the barking—oh, my goodness gracious—I don't even know what to say about it. No longer is it the cute little whine that used to escape his mouth as a puppy. No—it's this howling roar that seems to be endless. In addition to all this, I just have not been successful in the potty training area. Not only do I come home to potty disasters, but he's now taken to chewing the floor. I didn't think it would be possible, but he's actually peeled the tile off the kitchen floor and completely frayed the edge of the carpet. Won't this be lovely when company comes over! I have to be patient all day, and the last thing I want to be when I get home is patient. Sometimes I just wish I could wash my hands of him.

Lord, give me patience that will endure throughout my day. Please help me to concentrate on the joy my puppy brings me and not the craziness. Fill me with unending love so I can care for him with all of my heart. He is, after all, a true blessing from You. Forgive me for ever wanting to let him go.

• Man's Best Friends •

Puppy School

Yippee! It is time for doggie training school. My precious angel is nine months old now, and it is definitely time for some obedience lessons. What gave me the clue? Hmmmm. That's a tough one. Let me think . . . well, you know all the behaviors I mentioned before—chewing, pottying in the house, barking, jumping—none of them has improved. Not even one! I don't know how I thought puppies learned to behave, but whatever approach or lack thereof that I have been taking certainly has been ineffective up until now. So I've invested in a training seminar. It is a two-week program; he will be away for two whole weeks. Hee-hee. OOPS, I mean, that just makes me terribly sad. Actually, I will miss him very much, but I am excited about the prospect of being able to communicate with him effectively when he returns home. Truthfully, I think the school is as much for me as for him. Perhaps now I will be able to maintain some discipline in my household. I think it will be a benefit to us both.

Lord, give my precious puppy a big hug for me while he is away so he knows I love him. Help me to be dedicated to his training when he comes back so we can both be disciplined and learn together. Thank You for giving me his companionship. He is a true gift, and I love him. Please help me never to lose sight of that.

• Man's Best Friends •

Feline Fits

My cat is without a doubt the sweetest, most lovable cat on earth. All of this stuff about cats wanting to be their own boss, blah, blah, blah, well none of it is true about my cat. He comes when he's called, he rolls over and lets me rub his tummy, he gives little kitty kisses, and he likes nothing better than to curl up asleep in my lap. Not your typical cat. But then . . . the trip to the vet. I know you're saying to yourself that your cat is just as bad. I think not! It was time for the yearly shots, and I thought I was being sneaky by getting out the pet carrier and keeping it in the laundry room. Wrong! The growls began. Apparently, the odor of the vet clinic is so potent that it has the ability to call to the cat from rooms away. Yes, rooms! I'm talking like five rooms. So I figured that the surprise approach wouldn't work. I'd just put him in and get it over with; of course, I couldn't pick him up because he had already turned into bobcat pet. I had to attempt the grab-him-around-the-back-with-a-towel trick (and keep my face as far away as possible in the process, I might add). All right! He was in . . . so I thought. Not minutes later I returned for the carrier, and what did I see but a huge hole torn in the side. Yes, it was one of the cardboard kinds, not the plastic. So we went through the process again, but this time he was no longer bobcat kitty. He had turned into tiger cat. Hoping the duct tape would hold, I somehow got him into the carrier and to the vet. Then came the real task. The shots. Well, forget it. The vets wouldn't even touch him. Rrriiieeeooowww! Quite a scary sound for a little kitty that was no longer tiger cat but little ferocious lion-like monster! To make a long story short, they had to put the entire carrier into a plastic bag and gas the cat just to get him calm enough for the tranquilizer shot. Yikes! What an ordeal. He hated me for days. Yet eventually I was forgiven, and he became my loving, precious kitty again.

Father God, thank You for the many animals that bless our lives. Help them to forgive us for the trials we put them through, and help us to understand that they cannot control their fear. Thank You for their constant love and devotion. I think that maybe people could learn something from pets. They don't stop loving, even in the hard times. Thank You for that.

• Man's Best Friends •

Dog Owner Don'ts

I recently acquired new next-door neighbors. They moved in just before winter set in, and they have a cute, although somewhat disheveled dog. He really is a sweet thing, but I feel a bit sorry for him. They seemingly do not think it important to take him for walks. Now if you live somewhere with a backyard, perhaps this is not important. However, when your only yard is the sidewalk, it seems rather thoughtless—to many parties involved. Instead of walking him, they attach him to a leash and let him sit outside. Of course, he proceeds to go about his business all over the sidewalk. Lovely. Sometimes we get several little packages left on the sidewalk in one day, which is even more delightful. Aw, come on . . . gross! Pick up the poop! At least that's what I hear myself screaming in my head each time I walk outside my apartment. Ugh. What a mess. I've finally become accustomed to playing "dodge the doodoo" when I open my door, and at least they pick it up once every day or so. Well, all that changed once the snow came. We've had a very snowy winter here, and our sidewalks have become layers of frozen snow and ice. It was beautiful at first, but there's one huge problem that is reducing that beauty rather quickly. It seems that my neighbors do not see the need to do their pick-up duties in the snow. We have dozens of frozen brown piles speckled over our sidewalk. Most of them are probably fossilized in the snow by now, but they're visible enough to make me say "ew" each time I walk in or out of my house. Now, really. I don't want to be a nosy neighbor, and I certainly don't want to be rude. BUT—this is a definite dog owner DON'T! What do I do?

Lord, please help me to find the tact to say what I need to say in a diplomatic way. Please help them to hear me in the way it is intended. I want us all to enjoy our homes and the space around them. I want to welcome people to my house without having to apologize for the grotesque greeting. Lord, I ask Your guidance in this situation, and I ask You to help me be aware of how my behavior affects those around me.

• Man's Best Friends •

Tub Time

Today was one of those gray snow-melting days. It was nice enough, however, to go for a walk with the pup . . . at least that's what I thought. We started on our journey and met a friend along the way. Our excursion turned into a much longer one than I had planned. If you have lived in snowy places, then you're accustomed to what happens when the snow begins to melt. It transforms from piles of beautiful white powder into slowly disappearing heaps of brown mush. Ugh! It's not one of the loveliest times of year, but it is promising that spring is around the corner. Anyway—on this particular day, the snow seemed to be melting terribly quickly. It was impossible to keep the dog out of the dirty heaps. By the end of our walk, he was covered from head to toe in mud. Yikes. Having no hose for spraying him off and no yard to do it in, I was in a bit of a pickle. Hmmm. Well, the bathtub seemed the only viable route to take. I coaxed him into the bathroom with a bone and shut the door. Getting him into the bathtub took a series of attempts, but finally I had him in. Of course I had no dog shampoo, so I was going to have to use my Pantene. All seemed to go well initially . . . I ran just a bit of water so that I could lather him up. Except for the fact that I basically had to sit in the tub with him to keep him still, all was going surprisingly well. He was soaped up and ready for rinsing. Now here is where I should have planned more carefully. I thought to myself about the best way to rinse him off, and the shower seemed most logical. I turned it on, and the hysteria began. It seems my dog doesn't care for the shower. At the first pelts of water, he jumped straight up and out of the tub. He then, of course, shook himself off, spraying the entire bathroom with Pantene suds. Lovely! I, too, was covered from head to toe and not terribly pleased. There was no way I was letting him out of the bathroom that way, so I had to finish what I had started. With him struggling the whole time, I lifted my 50-pound pup back into the tub and held him still with the sheer force of all my body's strength. I pointed the shower head in his direction and tried to maneuver him around until all of the soap had been rinsed away and he was mud-free. What a mess. He was sparkling fresh, but the bathroom and I needed some serious cleaning.

Lord, what a day! Perhaps You might help me to think before I act next time—to foresee the potential results of my actions. I can't stop taking my pup on walks, but we'll have to find some alternative to the shower bathing method. I love him, Lord. Help me to be grateful for his presence in my life all the time, even on messy days like these. He truly is a bundle of joy, even when he's a bundle of muddy joy. Help me always to remember that.

Around the World

"By day the Lord went ahead of them in a pillar of cloud to guide them on their way and by night in a pillar of fire to give them light, so that they could travel by day or night."

Exodus 13:21

Loving Father, I thank You for guiding me on my travels as You guided the Israelites so many years ago. Although the clouds and fire may not be visible to the naked eye, I know that You are constantly directing me and leading me in my ventures. I am in awe of Your presence, Lord, and I am so blessed to have You travel with me. Not only are You with me when I set foot away from home, but You fill me with Your presence every day, making each new day a journey that we take together.

The Sardine Sleeper

My sister and I had the amazing opportunity to spend five weeks traveling in Europe this summer. We each brought one backpack and set off on our glorious adventure. Our first experience with a sleeper train was the trip between Amsterdam and Munich. It was quite a long haul and full of surprises. My sister and I turned sideways to squeeze into the train compartment, and once in, we discovered a sitting room that must have been smaller than the guest bath in our parents' house. We had our choice of six seats—three on one side facing the three on the other. We chose two seats next to each other, and my sister sat next to the window. The train was overcrowded, so eventually we had four men join us in our compartment. Two were college students, and two were older men returning home to Germany. Conversation came easily, and it was not until well after midnight that someone in the compartment deigned it sleep time. To our undisguised horror, we discovered that the seats in which we were relaxing folded down into a six-person sleeper sofa. Fancy that—how comfy. The same space that was a moment ago holding three people across now held six people squished person-to-person without even an inch of space in-between. My sister wisely placed herself against the window. I was next to her, and on the other side of me was

• Around the World •

one of the older men. He fell asleep quickly and proceeded to snore without control. Then, in sleep, his feet began to wander. Yuck! He was much too close, and I couldn't seem to get away. We were packed in like a can of sardines, and sucking in my bottom was not giving me any space. I was forced to squeeze closer to my sister, and I know the poor thing was kissing the wall. However, if I had to choose between squishing her and touching Mr. Footsie, she lost.

Dear God, thank You for enabling me to experience new adventures. Thank You for my sister, who keeps me sane and makes me laugh. Please help me to be understanding when I'm in awkward positions, and help me to know how to deal with the situations I face. Thank You for promising that something good will come from everything, and thank You for helping me find it.

• Frances Leary •

Read the Label

While my sister and I were on our European adventure, halfway through the trip we had depleted a large portion of our medical supplies. I had packed every kind of cold medicine I thought we would need, and we had consumed almost everything. While we were thoroughly enjoying our trip, our throats and noses were paying the price for our gallivanting around from climate to climate. Our coughing, especially, was becoming a disturbing problem to those around us, as well as ourselves. We stopped at a pharmacy in the Florence train station. Luckily, we had our Italian translation book with us. Without too much difficulty, we were able to purchase a bottle of cough medicine. Yea! Now we could enjoy the train ride without constant hacking. We got on the train, and each swallowed two tablespoons of the red liquid. The next thing I remember, in what seemed like only moments later, the train was at a stop. I nearly had to pry my eyes open to look over and see that my sister was still asleep. I picked my head up only to find that I had drooled over my entire pillow. Lovely. The train was almost empty, and I inquired about the name of the stop. Yikes! It was our stop, and we had a train to catch. I woke up my sister, peeled her from her pillow, and ran with her to find our connecting train. We made it just a minute before it pulled out

• Around the World •

of the station. Only then did I look at the label on the bottle of cough medicine. Yes, I was certain that the Italian word for codeine was listed as one of the ingredients. I suppose that would explain the nonstop four-hour nap and overzealous drooling. Next time I'll have to read the label first.

Lord, thank You for waking me in time for us to catch our train. Thank You, too, for the gentle lesson in reading directions. Thank You for keeping us safe and well, even though we don't seem to cooperate all the time. Please continue to watch over us while we're awake and as we sleep.

• Frances Leary •

The Drugstore Language Barrier

Still on our travels in Europe, my sister and I ran out of cough drops. This time we were in Greece, and we did not have any translation guide for Greek. Even if we did, I'm not sure it would help since the letters they use are entirely different from the characters in the alphabet as we know it. So neither of us speaking any Greek and without a communication guide in hand, we went to a drugstore in Athens, sorely in need of cough drops. The pharmacist, of course, spoke no English. What a pickle. There I was standing in the middle of the store making coughing noises and pointing to my throat. Then I attempted to appear like I was sucking on something, and I think I only succeeded in looking absolutely ridiculous. My sister wasn't helping at all because she was so busy laughing at me. The pharmacist pulled out some kind of antiseptic ointment. Yikes! What part of that goes with coughing and sucking? That just made my sister laugh even harder. Okay, so I had to try again. This time I pointed into my mouth, thinking that would let him know I needed something that would go inside my mouth. He looked perplexed, so I again made coughing noises to give him a hint. Poor man. I don't know how he deciphered my sign language, but finally he pulled a bag of cough drops from the drawer. I've never seen anyone so relieved to see a customer go.

Lord, thank You for helping us to find a way to a pharmacist who did not throw us out on our ears when we started behaving like lunatics. The world is full of good, generous people who want to help even those they cannot understand. Thank You for seeing us through the situation, and thank You for allowing us to laugh.

• Frances Leary •

The Last Train Ride

    The last train ride for my sister and me was from Barcelona to Paris. This time we had invested in a sleeper car so that each of us would actually have a bed. Yea! We found our designated cabin and quickly claimed our bunks. There were three bunks on one side and three on the other. I took one of the top bunks to be near the window, and my sister took the one beneath me. We were joined very quickly by a French woman and her son. As soon as I had climbed into bed, the little boy began playing. Up the steps, down the steps. Up the steps, down the steps. This continued for quite a while until I let out an audible sigh and his mother told him to stop. But, it wasn't over yet. Open the door, close the door. Open the door, close the door. Once this phase passed, it was up the steps, down the steps again. Then he found the window. Open the window, close the window. Open the window, close the window. This I could NOT handle! I become terribly claustrophobic without air circulation, and I began to have difficulty breathing. I asked the woman if she could please keep him from playing with the window. I don't think she understood my English, but she did stop him from playing with the window. Then it was up the steps, down the steps again. GOOD NIGHT! I was beginning to question my sanity about returning

Around the World

to my job with children in the fall. At the next stop a Frenchman who, thankfully, had no children joined us. Before he climbed into bed, he quickly, without asking anyone, shut the window. I attempted to resist the anxiety attack that was coming, and I cradled my inhaler to no avail. I then, just as quickly, reopened the window. A moment later he stood up and shut the window. It was like a scene in a silent movie. I sat up and explained to him the situation, only to find that he was very unwilling to negotiate. Never mind me—I'll just hyperventilate, have an asthma attack, and FREAK OUT! We finally called the porter. I got a different cabin, but my poor sister was left there to be awakened by up the steps, down the steps.

Lord, thank You for helping me get out of that horrible situation. I love children, but really. Please give me patience to tolerate people I think are difficult. Help me to love and respect them even when I don't understand their actions. Above all, help me to be less difficult for others.

Cuban Kayak Crisis

Recently, I joined three friends on an excursion to visit a friend working in Guantanamo Bay, Cuba. It was truly an adventure, and I think just the opportunity to say I went to Cuba was enough for me. We spent our days snorkeling, sightseeing, walking the beaches, and playing golf. One day our host decided to take us on a "short" kayak jaunt across the bay. Okay—I'm up for anything, but I had never ridden in a kayak in my life. I was a bit nervous, but there didn't seem to be anything to it. Basically, you move your arms to circulate the paddles, and away you go. Yeah, right! I had no idea what I was getting myself into. My friends who were with me had all had experience with canoeing or kayaking, and they were all much more athletic than I have ever been. They said it would be easy—no problem—so, off we went. Now I knew I was not She-Ra, Princess of Power, but I had never considered myself to be Little Miss Muffet, either. There I was, only halfway to the other side, the recipient of many fun-loving splashes from my friends, and I was embarrassingly fatigued. I have no doubt that my face was bright red, almost purple, and I was drenched in sweat (not from a good workout but from complete exhaustion). That thing about women glistening—whatever! I felt how I imagine a horse would feel after running the Kentucky Derby. My arms started to charley horse, and there was nothing to do but keep going. By this point, most of my friends had reached the other side, and I was barely past the middle. Too embarrassing for words. When I finally made it, they had to pull me onto the beach. I very awkwardly stumbled from the kayak and proceeded to lie on the beach breathing very audibly. Thankfully, my friends were too kind to make fun of me to my face (until later, that is). I don't think I've ever felt so inadequate in my entire life—that is, until the return trip.

Lord, thank You for humbling me. We all have our strengths, and kayaking definitely is not one of mine. In the future please help me to relax and have fun even when I'm not at my best. I especially thank You for friends who love me, even when I look ridiculous, and treasure me for who I am.

Still Dating

"Love is patient, love is kind. It does not envy, it does not boast, it is not proud. It is not rude, it is not self-seeking, it is not easily angered, it keeps no record of wrongs. Love does not delight in evil but rejoices with the truth. It always protects, always trusts, always hopes, always perseveres. Love never fails."
1 Corinthians 13:4–8

Lord God, thank You for Your presence in my life. I believe that one day You will guide me to the person who will be my partner in life, whom I will love unconditionally and who will love me unconditionally in return. Until then, I thank You for patience as I enjoy my life as a single person. Please guide my thoughts and my actions, so I may live a life that reflects Your will. I pray that the progress of my relationships will honor You.

Concert Stand-up

Wooh! I had just bought tickets to see Phil Collins perform in concert. How cool is that? I had actually been dating this guy for a little while (well, we'd had a few dates, anyway), so I thought it would be a great night for us. The concert was going to be an outdoor performance—how awesome to listen to good music under the stars and share it with someone who had some definite potential in the relationship department. I was so excited. We had planned to meet at his apartment and go from there. The concert started at 8:00 and was about an hour away. We decided to leave at 6:30 so we would have plenty of time, but when 6:30 came, he was nowhere to be found. Hmmm. Isn't this a bit annoying?! 6:45 and still no sign. Where could he be? By 7:00, I was in a fairly foul mood, but more than anything I was worried. Surely there had to be a reason for his lateness. 7:15, 7:30, still no date. Yikes. 7:45, 8:00 . . . nothing! The concert had started, and there I was standing outside on my date's doorstep an hour away from where I needed to be. This wasn't the type of concert pavilion to go to by myself, and it was too late to invite anyone else to go with me. What a bummer. I missed seeing Phil Collins because my date forgot about our plans. That's what he said the next day, anyway. I decided he had much less potential in the relationship department than I had originally thought. I just wish I hadn't had to miss Phil Collins to realize it.

Lord, what a disappointment—not just the concert, but the guy. I know that You are looking out for me as I make my choices. Please help me to see Your guidance and to act accordingly. Thank You for showing me that this man was not meant for me. I want to find someone special, and I trust that You have someone special picked out just for me. I know You will reveal all in Your time. Please help me to be patient.

• Frances Leary •

The Dr. Jekyll/Mr. Hyde Date

Holy cow! What did I get myself into? I agreed to a dinner date with a man who works with me. Perhaps that was my first mistake—never mix business with pleasure. *What harm can it be*, I thought. Boy, was I wrong. The first dinner was deceivingly lovely. Little did I know about his other side. Since we worked together, I saw this man on a regular basis. He would stop by and say "hello" numerous times throughout the day. It seemed friendly at first, but then it started to freak me out. Obsession took him over at some point, and he was absolutely sold on the fact that we were "together" in a relationship. I assured him that although we had a nice dinner, we were not "dating" each other. Obviously, I was not direct enough for him to understand. It made it more awkward when we went out with friends from work, and he would make sure to sit close to me and inevitably behave in an overly friendly manner. Ugh! Well, it was on one of those occasions that his alter ego appeared. As always he had arranged to be sitting in a chair next to mine. As the evening progressed, he attempted to put his arm around me multiple times. Each time I would shift in my seat or get up to speak with someone nearby. This apparently did not deter him. His attempts shifted to holding my hand. Yuck, not to mention very uncomfortable. By this time I was a bit creeped out by the guy. About the fifth time I withdrew my hand from his, he lost it—and I mean lost it! I've never seen anything like it. Not only did he raise his voice, but he started yelling at me so that all in the room turned their heads. He used a plethora of foul words during his explosion, and needless to say, I was rather taken aback. My friends had surrounded me by this time to ensure that I was not hurt, and basically, I let him know that his behavior was unacceptable and embarrassing. At that point, he started crying uncontrollably and begging me to take him back. Yikes! We were never in a relationship to start with! While I did not want to be heartless, I realized that he had more problems than I could ever help to fix.

Lord, thank You for delivering me from that situation without any scars. I am proud of the way I handled myself during the entire ordeal, and I thank You for Your guidance. I ask that You watch over my crying, yelling, cussing friend. He needs Your help, Lord. I hope that You can help him find peace.

• Frances Leary •

Bingo Blues

Well, after that dating fiasco I decided I needed to lay low for a while. Perhaps if I didn't go looking for anything, then nothing weird would come looking for me. Boy, was I wrong. I was taking my dog for a walk one evening, when my neighbor caught up with me. He was a friend of a friend, so I saw no harm in walking with him. It was a beautiful, crisp winter night, and conversation came easily as we walked and tried to stay warm underneath all the winter layers. He called me a few days later to ask me out. We'd had a nice walk, so it sounded like fun. Well, I can honestly tell you that I have never been on a more bizarre date. He does not have a car, and I wasn't about to walk downtown in the middle of winter. Given that, I picked him up at his house. We went to play bingo at a local hall, which although initially sounding quaint, proved to be quite unenjoyable. In all fairness, perhaps I should give the game of bingo another chance. The awkwardness stemmed initially from my date's silence. He had seemed quite talkative on our evening walk, but apparently the "date" situation left him without words—almost completely. He spoke only when I spoke to him, and then he responded with simple one-word answers. Yikes. I was drowning. That was not the weirdest part, however. The weird part was the staring. He did

• Still Dating •

not take his eyes off me. Ordinarily, I might have taken this as a compliment. In this case, however, it was just very uncomfortable. He has these big eyes that seem to sink into oblivion when he stares. Combine that with the lack of conversation, and I can truly say that I did not feel one ounce of attraction toward him. Nice guy, but man, does he need to work on his dating skills. By that time it was raining, and I drove him home. He asked me to wait a minute and went inside. He returned with several red roses and asked if he could kiss me goodnight. Ugh. Sorry if any of you are still holding your breath on this one—I said no. What a weird night.

Lord, he seems like an awfully nice guy. There's definitely no attraction on my part, so I'm certain I did the right thing at the end of the evening. It's always so awful to be in such an awkward situation. Comfort him, Lord. I hope he has the opportunity to meet someone who does feel that attraction and will give him the chance to develop his communication further. I'm definitely not that girl, but I am thankful that You brought him to me on that cold night. It was a much more enjoyable walk, and I hope that perhaps I've found a friend.

• Frances Leary •

• Still Dating •

Love Letter

Okay—so I got this weird letter in the mail. No return address, of course, and I didn't recognize the handwriting. Ding, ding, ding . . . perhaps those facts should have set off some warning bells in my head, but trusting little me just opened the letter, tra, la, la. Well, inside was a passage I won't repeat. It wasn't exactly inappropriate, but it was so personal that it gave me the creeps. I do not have a relationship with anyone who is close enough for that type of poetry. Okay—now I'm freaked out. Who could have sent this? There's my neighbor two doors down, who always seems to watch me closely. There's the bingo guy, who is still fostering a bruised ego. There's another neighbor who drops by frequently and likes to give me hugs. Oh . . . Yuck! I hope this was a sincere gesture from someone trying to pay me a compliment, but I must admit to being rather shaken. How can a piece of mail make you want to take a shower?

Dear Lord, please help me to let this go. It's an experience I don't need to hold onto. Perhaps it was a misguided attempt to be a secret admirer, but it crossed the line. I pray for the sender of this letter. May Your spirit fill that person, whoever it is, and may Your wisdom be a guide always. I pray the sender will not cross the line of personal boundaries again—with me or with anyone else.

• Still Dating •

Broken Heart

With all this talk about dating, I bet you'd be surprised to know that in the back of my mind I've believed for years now that I knew the man I was going to marry. We've been friends for years—since high school. Actually, he was a high school boyfriend who then became my best friend. For the past several years we've done everything together—so much so that all of our friends ask when we're finally going to break down and realize that we're just meant to be together. Even though we both have dated people sporadically the past several years and have never crossed over the friendship line with each other, I've believed that he was the one for me. How wrong I was. I had a dream one night, and I knew that he had started dating someone—not just someone, but his future wife. He told me the day after my dream that he had begun a relationship with someone—I guessed her name before he could say it. For years I had been holding back, waiting for the perfect moment to share with him my true feelings. This wasn't the way I had it planned, but I poured out myself to him, hoping in vain to hold onto the façade I had conjured in my mind as truth. He held me, admitting to having had feelings for me at times. At this time, however, his heart was with another. Even with this knowledge, I hung onto the dream for a while, hoping this was all some silly deviation off his true path. Apparently, it wasn't. They're engaged now. The wedding is planned for next year. I suppose it is time that I truly moved on.

Lord, if this man is not the one for me, why was my life intertwined so closely with his for so long? Why did all of our friends insist that we belonged together? I don't understand. I have faith that You know what You're doing. I believe in You and in the path that You have chosen for me. I believe that if this man is not my soul mate, then there is another more incredible than I can imagine. Help me to be patient, Lord, and always to trust in Your will and follow Your ways. Sometimes it is hard, Lord, but I feel as if finally I can truly begin to live without that shadow in the back of my mind—the shadow which falsely tells me that he is the one for me. You've removed that shadow, Lord. Thank You for freeing me from my own self-made constraints. Thank You for helping me to trust You—always!

Friends and Family

"Love must be sincere. Hate what is evil; cling to what is good. Be devoted to one another in brotherly love. Honor one another above yourselves. Never be lacking in zeal, but keep your spiritual fervor, serving the Lord. Be joyful in hope, patient in affliction, faithful in prayer. Share with God's people who are in need. Practice hospitality. Bless those who persecute you; bless and do not curse. Rejoice with those who rejoice; mourn with those who mourn. Live in harmony with one another. Do not be proud, but be willing to associate with people of low position. Do not be conceited. Do not repay anyone evil for evil. Be careful to do what is right in the eyes of everybody. If it is possible, as far as it depends on you, live at peace with everyone."

Romans 12:9–18

Thank You, God, for the gift of community. I am so blessed by the love of my friends and the love of my family. There are times when we fail one another, but our love does not fail because You are the foundation. I pray that my love for others and communications with others may be a testimony to Your love, and I pray that all Your children may live in harmony and peace.

• Friends and Family •

Wedding Worries

Yikes! I have yet another wedding to attend this weekend. Beautiful dresses, heavenly flowers, music, dancing, commitments, vows, smiles, tears—it's enough to drive a person crazy. Here I am, and I should be completely happy for my friends as they celebrate their love for each other. Instead, I find my mind preoccupied, and the tears of happiness I shed when I think of the bride become tears of pity for myself. In the last year, I must have been to at least ten weddings. It seems as if all my friends are tying the knot. On top of that, many of the newlyweds are even younger than I am. Aaahhh! I am happy for them, but inside I feel bitter. When is it going to be my turn? I know that it will happen when the time is right, but sometimes I really want to know when that will be. (Psst . . . By the way, God, just in case You were wondering, it would be okay with me if that time were now.) At the moment, however, I do not have one prospect, and I become discouraged. Actually, I become downright doubtful. I know that God hasn't overlooked me, but I feel overlooked. I know that when it comes, it will be perfect, but how can I possibly wait 50 years? Okay, so I'm hoping it's not actually going to be 50 years.

Lord, please fill me with joy for my friends who

have found someone with whom to share their lives. Bless them as they begin their new lives together with You. Help me to be patient until the time is right for me. Fill my heart with gladness for the time I have to spend with You and myself. Help me not to look so much to the future, but to concentrate on doing Your will in the present. I have faith that You have someone very special in store for me. Father, please keep that faith strong.

• Friends and Family •

Birthday Blues

Well, my birthday is today. Yup, I'm definitely another year older, and I'm now officially well into the mid-twenties. I didn't expect a brass band marching outside my house, and I knew that three dozen long-stemmed roses was probably a long shot. However, I have to admit that I did kind of expect a phone call or two. You know—phone call—that thing that friends do to let one another know they care. At least, that's what I thought friends did with the phone. Apparently not. I waited and waited and waited and waited. I had a lovely evening and a superb dinner with my parents, but I cannot deny that I was hurt. I know that as we get older, we tend to lose touch and sometimes forget things like birthdays, but I realized tonight how important those days can be. The whole thing made me think of Christmas. Every year we celebrate the birthday of Jesus, but how many of us forget to do what's important? How many of us give presents without stopping to say "I love You, Lord?" I wonder how Christ feels when we forget His birthday.

Lord God, forgive me for resenting my friends this evening. Please help me not to place value on my friendships based on the events of one night. Also, Lord, help me to be more sensitive to the needs of my friends, so that when they come to a time of needing me, I will be there. Thank You for the amazing blessing of my parents. You knew what You were doing when You put us all together. What a treasure they are! Thank You above all, Lord, for the gift of Your Son. Please help me to remember to celebrate His life, not only on Christmas but every day I live.

• Friends and Family •

Catching a Lie

Hmmm . . . it seems that my best friend is not being honest with me. How do I know? He is keeping me very distant, and he is no longer sharing with me what is going on in his life. In addition to that, several times he has told me one thing but done something entirely different. This hurts me so much. This person is a friend I trust with everything in my life, and it is hard for me to accept that for the time being he does not feel that same way about me. We have been friends for many years, and our friendship has been getting much stronger—until now. I want to talk to him about this, but I think that might be rather selfish. Telling him that he is hurting me would only be hurting him in return. I do not want to do that; I simply want to understand. I wish I could just shout "liar, liar, pants on fire" and be done with it, but somehow I don't think that would help solve the problem one bit. I think it would be much easier if he were a woman. It's much easier for me to understand the actions of women, since I am one. This whole *Men are from Mars* thing adds an entirely new dimension to relationships as I know them. However, that does not change the fact that he is being dishonest, and I don't know what to do. I know he loves me, but right now I do not feel it all the time.

God, please give me the understanding to recognize that he is dealing with something in his life right now that he is not ready to share with me. For whatever the reasons that I do not understand, he needs some time to sort things out on his own. Help me to have patience to wait, faith to know that our friendship will last, and love for my friend that will withstand this and any trial. Thank You. Your love fulfills all my needs.

• Friends and Family •

Sister of the Bride

What a beautiful wedding! She was the perfect bride, so in love and happy. HELLO—I thought I was supposed to go first. You know, the OLDEST?! I kept waiting for my father to put the veil on my head and insist that I take my sister's place. I'm not sure the groom would accept that end of the deal, but, of course, he would have no choice. After all, she did break the tradition. Here I am, an old maid (okay, not really), and she's walking up the aisle to commit her life to someone she met less than a year ago. Ha! She's just a baby! Yet as I look at her, I see that somehow before my very eyes she has blossomed into a beautiful, intelligent, loving woman. When did she do that? I thought I was supposed to take care of her, watch out for her, protect her—I guess it's his job now, though I pass the torch rather regretfully. I know he'll do a great job, probably better than I can, but I can't help thinking I'm going to miss it.

Dear Lord, You know that she's my best friend in the world. Please bless their life together and walk with them as they walk side by side. Thank You for the beauty of their love and the example it is to others. Help me to follow their example and never settle for something less than right. In Your time, Lord, in Your time.

• Friends and Family •

True Love

I ran into my parents last night. I was having dinner at an Italian restaurant with some friends, and I looked up to see my parents waiting for a table. As they looked into each other's eyes, they were holding hands, and it was obvious to everyone that they were enjoying each other's company. More than that, it was impossible to miss that they were in love. They had spent the day on the beach walking and looking for seashells. I think more than anything they were taking the time out of their busy lives to spend time loving each other. They had a romantic dinner planned, and after that they were off to a movie. What a day! What a date! None of my dates recently have come even close to par. It's absolutely amazing to watch my parents as they watch each other, their eyes completely filled with understanding and compassion. Every moment they spend together seems to strengthen the love they share. They have been married 40 years now, and they continue to love each other more every day. What a blessing they are to me, and what a witness they are. Their relationship is a testimony that love exists and lasts. I know it's been a long road, and I know they have challenges that lie ahead. It's amazing to see that they are stronger for every obstacle they have overcome—40 years—and more in love than ever. I only hope I will be so blessed someday.

Thank You, Lord, for the gift of my parents. Thank You for their love for each other and their love for our family. I know You have that in store for me, Lord. Help me to be patient and put my life in Your hands. I know that love like that can only be found through You.

A Bend in the Road

"Trust in the Lord with all your heart and lean not on your own understanding; in all your ways acknowledge him, and he will make your paths straight.

Proverbs 3:5–6

Dear God, I come to a time when new paths arise before me. I ask for Your guidance, and I pray that I might discern Your will in my life. I defer my decisions to You, O Lord. You are my way, my truth, and my life. I will follow You.

• Frances Leary •

Saying Goodbyes

My band just finished our final concert. What a night. Melancholy seemed to hang in the air. I was crying, of course, but there's nothing unusual there. It was a good ride—two CDs and five great years. We just reached a point where we all wanted different things. As for me, I'm thankful for the experiences but ready to move on. I've lived in this city for seven years, ever since I moved back from college. I've made great friends and spent quality time with my very special family. Nevertheless, there's been something missing. Perhaps I'm missing a bit of myself. I think I've been trying to figure out for a long time what I really want to do with my life. Do I want to sing? Do I want to teach? I've done and loved them both for five years now, and yet here I am packing up a U-Haul and driving seven days across the country to live in Canada and go to graduate school. That's always been a dream of mine too—the graduate school part, that is. So I say goodbye to my family and friends. I know the kindred spirits will always be with me, but it will never be the same.

Lord, be with me as I embark upon this new journey. I don't know what it holds in store, but I know without a doubt that this is the path You have laid out for me. I'm excited, but I'm apprehensive to

• A Bend in the Road •

be in a strange city knowing no one but You. Thank You for being with me, Lord. What a ride this will be!

• Frances Leary •

A New Home

Here I am! Finally. It took me seven days of driving, but I'm here . . . on the eastern-most point of North America, I might add. St. John's, Newfoundland. What an amazing place—it's almost like stepping back in time. My apartment stands in a long row of multicolored wooden homes lining a narrow street of this old fishing town. It's much more than that, of course, and that is why I'm here. I remember when I first knew I was meant to come here. I was searching for universities that specialize in my field of folklore, and I found this one—Memorial University of Newfoundland. I gasped, ran to the map in my room, and started jumping up and down like a giddy schoolgirl. For that moment, I became Anne of Green Gables anticipating her return home. Yes, I know her home was Prince Edward Island, but Newfoundland is close enough! And here I am. I've been out for an evening stroll, watching the fog settle on the dimly-lighted streets. It's beautiful. School will begin soon, and I can't wait. I know I'll be challenged to think in ways I didn't know possible, and I welcome it. I feel like Julie Andrews in *The Sound of Music*, ready to sing "I have confidence" as I race to begin my new adventure. I'm here alone, and yet I'm not lonely. I'm filled with peace, and I can't wait to see what's in store.

• A Bend in the Road •

Lord, thank You for bringing me here. This place is magical in some way, and I can't wait to know it more. I trust that You have brought me here for a purpose, and I pray that I have the wisdom to follow Your guidance along the way. I love You, Lord, and I trust You to make straight my path! Thank You!

• Frances Leary •

A Smiling Stranger

It's funny how no matter where you go, your passions always find you. The learning I've been doing over the past months has been incredible—challenging, thought-provoking, inspiring—I've loved every minute of it. However, it seems that study is not all this place holds for me. I joined a band—this one is more traditional, but it's music that I simply can't resist. We met for the first time with our guitarist today. I was sitting on top of the table in my department's grad room, and there he was. He still had his winter coat on, and his hat was pulled down over his ears. Only a bit of his curly hair poked out underneath. And that smile—it stopped me breathless. Holy cow! There I was in a bulky sweater looking the furthest thing possible from my most attractive, but he looked at me all the same. It was as if his eyes could see right through me. Funny how things work . . . just when I stop looking for a man, he waltzes through the door and knocks my socks off. Where's this going? Who knows? But I can't wait to find out!

Lord, thank You for my new friend. If nothing else, I pray for that. However, if there is something else, Lord, I welcome it. I ask for the ability to know Your will in this situation and in all others. This one feels different, Lord. My trust is in You.

• A Bend in the Road •

Looking Back

A new phase of life now embraces me. As I look forward to all it holds, I pause first to reflect on all that has brought me here. For ten years I have lived the Christian single life, first in those crazy college years and later in those first years of independence through which I struggled to discover my own path. It's been an exciting road, and I have grown so much along the way. I know how to cook successfully now; I no longer burn every meal. In fact, my parents even asked me to cook for them and my grandmother a few months ago. What an accomplishment! I still haven't mastered the art of baking, but I've improved. Living on my own has taught me so much about taking care of myself and my home. I still have the occasional mishap with household appliances, but thankfully I've learned how most of them work. Although occasionally I take great pleasure in lounging around, I no longer feel that I am wasting my life as a couch potato. And thankfully, I've become a master of balancing my checkbook. What a relief! So many things have changed. I still struggle with the fitness challenge, but with my cooking knowledge has come an enjoyment of eating at home. It saves money, and it's healthier—definitely a winning combo. Dating remains a mystery, but perhaps my prospects are looking up. Only God knows.

Lord, over the past ten years since I left my parents' home to make a life on my own, You have been my guide and inspiration. You have taught me so many lessons about life, and You have helped me to listen even when I remained closed to Your word. I have learned so much by allowing myself to hear the wisdom You offer me. It feels as if I'm leaving my young single life behind. I don't know what's ahead, but I'm a more confident woman now, ready to embrace the future. Help me always to hear Your words, to see Your face in those around me, and to follow Your will in my life. Thank You for continuing to show me the way!

Contact Frances Leary
or order more copies of this book at

TATE PUBLISHING, LLC

127 East Trade Center Terrace
Mustang, Oklahoma 73064

(888) 361 - 9473

Tate Publishing, LLC

www.tatepublishing.com